AF174032

Clarissa's Closet

By

MONICA LONG ROSS

Music and Lyrics by

ALAN RUCH

Dramatic Publishing Company

Woodstock, Illinois ● Australia ● New Zealand ● South Africa

*** NOTICE ***

The amateur and stock acting rights to this work are controlled exclusively by THE DRAMATIC PUBLISHING COMPANY, INC., without whose permission in writing no performance of it may be given. Royalty must be paid every time a play is performed whether or not it is presented for profit and whether or not admission is charged. A play is performed any time it is acted before an audience. Current royalty rates, applications and restrictions may be found at our website: www. dramaticpublishing.com, or we may be contacted by mail at: THE DRAMATIC PUBLISHING COMPANY, INC., 311 Washington St., Woodstock, IL 60098.

COPYRIGHT LAW GIVES THE AUTHOR OR THE AUTHOR'S AGENT THE EXCLUSIVE RIGHT TO MAKE COPIES. This law provides authors with a fair return for their creative efforts. Authors earn their living from the royalties they receive from book sales and from the performance of their work. Conscientious observance of copyright law is not only ethical, it encourages authors to continue their creative work. This work is fully protected by copyright. No alterations, deletions or substitutions may be made in the work without the prior written consent of the publisher. No part of this work may be reproduced or transmitted in any form or by any means, electronic or mechanical, including photocopy, recording, videotape, film, or any information storage and retrieval system, without permission in writing from the publisher. It may not be performed either by professionals or amateurs without payment of royalty. All rights, including, but not limited to, the professional, motion picture, radio, television, videotape, foreign language, tabloid, recitation, lecturing, publication and reading, are reserved.

For performance of any songs, music and recordings mentioned in this play which are in copyright, the permission of the copyright owners must be obtained or other songs and recordings in the public domain substituted.

© 1992 by
MONICA LONG ROSS & ALAN RUCH

© 1996 by
ANCHORAGE PRESS, INC.

Printed in the United States of America
All Rights Reserved
(CLARISSA'S CLOSET)

ISBN: 978-0-87602-343-3

IMPORTANT BILLING AND CREDIT REQUIREMENTS

All producers of the play *must* give credit to the author of the play in all programs distributed in connection with performances of the play and in all instances in which the title of the play appears for purposes of advertising, publicizing or otherwise exploiting the play and/or a production. The name of the author *must* also appear on a separate line, on which no other name appears, immediately following the title, and *must* appear in size of type not less than fifty percent (50%) the size of the title type. Biographical information on the author, if included in the playbook, may be used in all programs. *In all programs this notice must appear:*

"Produced by special arrangement with
THE DRAMATIC PUBLISHING COMPANY, INC., of Woodstock, Illinois."

Acknowledgment

The musical version of CLARISSA'S CLOSET was originally produced by Childsplay, Inc. of Tempe, Arizona.

PETER: THAT'S JUST AS WELL
WE DON'T WANT CHILDREN STOPPING BY
THIS ROOM IS ONLY SUITED FOR A
COCKROACH OR A FLY.

AND THEN THERE'S GRANDMA
SHE WILL BE HERE SOON
FOR A VISIT
AND YOUR CLOSET SMELL IS NOT
A HEALTHY KIND OF WELCOME, IS IT?
POOR GRANDMA'S OLD NOW
SHE'S ON HER LAST LEGS
PROB'LY LAME, TOO
AND A SMELL LIKE THAT
WILL KNOCK HER FLAT
AND EV'RY-ONE WILL BLAME YOU.

CLARISSA: *(Spoken.)* There he is men, that cowardly villain, the
Sheriff of Nottingham!

PETER: HOW CAN YOU LIVE LIKE A PIG
HOW CAN YOU BE SUCH A SLOB
YOUR CLOSET'S A MESS
AND THE SMELL HAS BECOME
SO SICK'NING I GUESS THAT YOUR NOSE MUST BE
NUMB
HOW CAN YOU LIVE LIKE A PIG, CLARISSA?
HOW CAN YOU LIVE LIKE A PIG?

MERRY MEN: *(Sung with Peter)*
SEIZE HIM AND TETHER HIM
TAR HIM AND FEATHER HIM
HEIGH-HO! HE'S GOT TO GO
SHERIFF OF NOTTINGHAM MEET YOUR FOE.

PETER: HOW CAN SHE LIVE LIKE A PIG?
HOW CAN SHE BE SUCH A SLOB?
HER CLOSET'S A MESS AND THE SMELL HAS
BECOME

8

CHARACTERS

CLARISSA   a 10-12 year old girl

PETER   Her younger brother

MOM

DAD

GRANDMA

CLOSET
CHARACTERS   Characters from Clarissa's imagination

The play has been produced with as few as 5 and with as many as 12 actors.

SETTING

The play takes place in Clarissa's messy bedroom which contains, along with the usual (or perhaps not so usual) bedroom furniture, a most unusual closet.

The musical score may be obtained from Anchorage Press, Inc.

(Music begins and plays under beginning. CLARISSA's room is seen - - it's a mess. CLARISSA enters and begins searching for her earmuffs.)

CLARISSA: I don't smell anything.

(MOM enters with large trash can. CLARISSA hides.)

MOM: Clarissa? Clarissa? *(SHE gets no answer.)* Clarissa. Dad? *(DAD enters.)* Clarissa.

DAD: Now, Clarissa . . .

(PETER enters. HE shouts.)

PETER: CLARISSA! !

DAD AND MOM: Peter.

(CLARISSA has found her earmuffs which SHE puts on cue "Peter." CLARISSA begins song. MOM and DAD and PETER are accustomed to her going into her own world. They wait until they have a chance to break in.)

I LIKE IT LIKE THIS

CLARISSA: *(Spoken)* I'll pretend I'm a lady
Who is very, very rich.
(Sung) I'D BUY A GREAT BIG CASTLE
WHERE A PRINCESS USED TO STAY
WITH A DUNGEON IN THE BASEMENT
AND A TOWER IN THE ATTIC.
THE CROCODILES FLOATING IN THE MOAT
WOULD KEEP AWAY
ANY MOTHERS, DADS OR BROTHERS
WHO WOULD COME TO GIVE ME STATIC.
I'D SPEND MY DAYS WITH KNIGHTS
WHEN THERE'S A BATTLE TO CONCOCT
FROM MY BALCONY, AT THREE,

1

CLARISSA: I'D GIVE A SPEECH TO ALL MY PEASANTS
AND THEN, AT MAYBE FOUR O'CLOCK
I'D HAVE THE IRON DOOR UNLOCKED
ALLOWING THE COWTOWING
AND THE SHOWERING OF PRESENTS.
THEN WHEN I'M ALONE,
I GATHER ALL THE PRESENTS
WHICH THE PEASANTS BROUGHT TODAY
AND PUT THEM WITH THE OTHERS
THAT THEY GAVE MY YESTERDAY
SOON I KNOW MY SEVERAL THOUSAND
TREASURES, ALL IN ALL
WILL ADD UP TO A GIANT STACK
THAT MEASURES WALL TO WALL.
SO WHAT
IF MY CASTLE'S JUST
A LITTLE BIT CROWDED
SO WHAT
IF THERE'S HARDLY EVEN
ROOM ENOUGH TO PLAY
I CAN'T DO WITHOUT IT
THERE'S NO DOUBT ABOUT IT.
I LIKE IT THIS WAY.

(MOM and DAD lift up the earmuffs and sing.)

MOM: *(Sung with Dad's and Peter's verses.)*
CLARISSA, DEAR, YOU MUST CONFESS
YOUR CLOSET IS AN AWFUL MESS
AND NOT EXACTLY ODORLESS
THIS PROBLEM WILL NOT GO
UNLESS YOU ACQUIESCE
TO NOW ADDRESS YOUR KNACK,
I GUESS FOR CARELESSNESS.
I STRESS THIS MAD OUTRAGEOUSNESS
IS LESS THAN ADVANTAGEOUSNESS.
CLARISSA, CLEAN UP YOUR ROOM.

2

DAD: CLARISSA, ANGEL
                CLARISSA DEAR
                IT'S JUST A DAY 'TILL YOUR GRANDMA'S HERE.
                CLARISSA, PUMPKIN,
                YOUR MOTHER THINKS,
                MY LITTLE MONKEY,
                YOUR CLOSET STINKS.
                CLARISSA, CLEAN UP YOUR ROOM.

PETER: CLARISSA, CLARISSA
                CLARISSA, CLARISSA
                CLARISSA, CLARISSA
                CLARISSA, CLARISSA
                CLARISSA!

MOM and DAD: Peter!

MOM: Just tidy up a bit.

DAD: Do it for Grandma.

PETER: Or she'll come for a visit and die.

MOM AND DAD: Peter.

                (CLARISSA puts the earmuffs back on and continues song.)

I LIKE IT LIKE THIS #2

CLARISSA: *(Spoken.)* I'll pretend I was kidnapped by a monster

                (Sung.) HE'D BE A GREAT BIG, UGLY-LOOKING
                BEAST WITH LOTS OF HAIR
                (MONSTER enters.)
                HE'S ANGRY AS A HORNET
                SO HE'S GROWLING LIKE A BEAR.

3

CLARISSA: I RAN AS FAST AS I COULD GO,
             COMPARED TO HIM, I RAN TOO SLOW.
             HE CAUGHT ME AND HE KNOCKED ME OUT
             AND TOOK ME TO HIS LAIR.
             WHEN I WOKE UP
             I FOUND THAT I WAS DEEP INSIDE A CAVE.
             THAT MONSTER CHAINED ME TO A ROCK,
             SO I WOULD ALWAYS BE HIS SLAVE.
             THE CAVE WAS VERY DARK
             SO I COULD HARDLY EVEN SEE
             I REALLY WAS CONCERNED
             THAT I MIGHT NEVER BE SET FREE.
             THEN WHEN THE BEAST CAME IN
             HE BUILT A LITTLE FIRE IN THE CENTER OF THE
             ROOM.
             IT LIT UP THE ENTIRE CAVE WITH TERRIFYING
             GLOOM.
             SHRUNKEN HEADS AND RATS
             AND MUSTY PLACES TURNING GREEN.
             IT REALLY WAS THE MOST DISGUSTING
             PLACE I'D EVER SEEN *(MONSTER growls.)*
             SO WHAT IF THE CAVE IS JUST A LITTLE BIT
             SICK'NING *(Growl.)*
             SO WHAT IF I'M SCARED THAT HE MIGHT
             KILL ME ANY DAY,
             HE CAN'T DO WITHOUT IT,
             THERE'S NO DOUBT ABOUT IT

MONSTER: I LIKE IT

CLARISSA: SO, I LIKE IT

BOTH: WE LIKE IT THIS WAY
                    (Removing her earmuffs)

MOM, DAD, and PETER: CLARISSA, PLEASE CLEAN UP YOUR
                      ROOM.

MOM and DAD: Fill the can, Clarissa.

4

PETER: And find the smell.

MOM and DAD: Peter.

                  *(MOM and DAD exit. PETER puts on gas mask as HE
                  approaches closet.)*

PETER: *(PETER speaks to CLARISSA using lots of gestures but
                  the mask makes it impossible to hear what he is saying.)*

CLARISSA: *(After listening to his speech.)* Get out, Peter.

PETER: *(Removes gas mask.)* Why do you need all this stuff,
                  Clarissa? Most of it is junk you can't even play with.

CLARISSA: I've told you a hundred million times, Peter. I don't
                  play - - I write. Now get out.

PETER: You have to do it, Clarissa. And I'm going to help. *(HE
                  walks toward the closet.)*

CLARISSA: You know you can't go in my closet, Peter.

PETER: Why, not?

CLARISSA: Do you know what I keep in my closet, Peter?

PETER: Something that smells bad.

CLARISSA: This closet is full of beasts and spiders and ghouls and
                  vampires. *(Growling and beast sounds of all sorts are
                  heard from the closet and they grow in intensity as
                  CLARISSA speaks.)* And they are very, very hungry.
                  So, if you open this door, they will tear you into little bitty
                  pieces.

PETER: There are no such things as vampires, Clarissa. *(The
                  sounds stop.)* All I want is my bowling ball. Do you have
                  it in there?

CLARISSA: Don' t you believe there are ferocious animals in my closet, Peter?

PETER: No.

CLARISSA: Do you want to find out? *(Faint beast sounds are heard.)*

PETER: I guess so.

CLARISSA: Are you willing to go in and see for yourself?

PETER: Well . . .

CLARISSA: What's the matter? Are you scared?

PETER: Of course not.

CLARISSA: Then go ahead. But, I warn you. *(PETER puts on gas mask and opens closet door. Beast and other magical sounds are heard. HE goes in slowly. Silence and a pause follows. Then a pounding is heard. CLARISSA opens the door and PETER emerges without gas mask and coughing.)*

PETER: *(Between coughs)* It's awful.

CLARISSA: What is? What did you see?

PETER: I couldn't see anything with this *(Indicating mask),* so I took it off. *(Remembering.)* Oh, dear. *(HE coughs.)*

CLARISSA: And then what happened? Did something attack you? Well, did it?

PETER: No one could live in there- - it's awful.

CLARISSA: I told you.

6

PETER: No, not that. I mean - - it stinks!

              (CLOSET growls. CLARISSA holds it back. PETER
              begins song. During song, CLARISSA whistles and
              MERRY MEN appear.)

              HOW CAN YOU LIVE LIKE A PIG?

PETER: HOW CAN YOU LIVE LIKE A PIG
              HOW CAN YOU BE SUCH A SLOB
              YOUR CLOSET'S A MESS
              AND THE SMELL HAS BECOME
              SO SICK'NING I GUESS THAT YOUR NOSE MUST BE
              NUMB
              HOW CAN YOU LIVE LIKE A PIG, CLARISSA?
              HOW CAN YOU LIVE LIKE A PIG?

              YOUR SMELL IS MORE DISGUSTING THAN A
              SKUNK'S
              IT'S EVEN WORSE THAN SWEATY SOCKS
              OR KITTY'S LITTER CHUNKS
              AND IF YOU FELL
              INTO THE SEWER GOODNESS KNOWS
              COMPARED TO WHAT'S IN THERE
              YOU'D COME OUT SMELLING LIKE A ROSE.

              HOW CAN YOU LIVE LIKE A PIG
              HOW CAN YOU BE SUCH A SLOB
              YOUR CLOSET'S A MESS
              AND THE SMELL HAS BECOME
              SO SICK'NING I GUESS THAT YOUR NOSE MUST BE
              NUMB
              HOW CAN YOU LIVE LIKE A PIG, CLARISSA?
              HOW CAN YOU LIVE LIKE A PIG?

              THAT SMELL KEEPS GETTING STRONGER EVERY
              DAY
              THE KIDS AROUND OUR NEIGHBORHOOD
              NO LONGER COME TO PLAY.

PETER: SO SICK'NING I GUESS THAT HER NOSE MUST BE
                NUMB
                HOW CAN YOU LIVE LIKE A PIG, CLARISSA?
                HOW CAN YOU LIVE LIKE A PIG?

MERRY MEN: *(Sung with Peter's verse)*
                OOH, THIS IS THE END FOR YOU
                OH, THIS SHERIFF HAS GOT TO GO
                CAN'T WAIT TO MUTILATE YOU
                PIG!
                HOW CAN YOU LIVE?
                WE'VE COME TOGETHER
                TO TAR AND TO FEATHER YOU

CLARISSA: *(Spoken.)* I warn you, Nottingham. You're not liked
                around here!

PETER: HOW CAN YOU LIVE LIKE A PIG?

MERRY MEN: *(Sung with Peter.)*
                YOU CANNOT LIVE
                YOU'RE A PIG!

                *(MERRY MEN push PETER off and exit into closet.
                THEY hesitate because of smell.)*

CLARISSA: I can't clean right now. I have to do my homework.

PETER: *(Off-stage.)* On Saturday - - Ha!

                *(CLARISSA sets herself up to do homework: gets
                notebooks and pencil and feigns concentration. SHE
                gets an idea. SHE speaks as she writes.)*

CLARISSA: Chapter 86: "Death on the High Seas." The sailors
                were swabbing the deck, hoisting the sails and singing a
                pirate song. *(PIRATES enter singing.)*

PIRATE SONG

PIRATES: WE'RE MEAN
            SO VERY MEAN
            WE KICK DOGS AND CATS
            AND TAKE CANDY FROM BABIES
            WE LIKE TO EAT GNATS AND WE
            THINK WE HAVE RABIES
            WE LOVE IT AND THAT'S WHY
            THERE'S NO IF'S OR MAYBE'S
            WE'RE OBSCENELY MEAN.

CLARISSA: *(Still writing.)* The ship rolled an pitched in the stormy
            seas. The wind, at gale force blew the sailors about like,
            like bowling balls. *(The PIRATES act out the image.
            CLARISSA rejects it.)* No, that's not right. The wind
            blew them around like dried old leaves. *(Again, acted
            out.)* . . . like dominoes? *(Acted out.)* No . . . the wind
            just blew them around the deck so that they could hardly
            stand still - - I'll work on that later. The sky looked
            ominous! All in all, it promised to be a bad day at sea.
            But, these tough sailors laughed into the wind *(The
            PIRATES laugh into the wind.)* because they were
            pirates, cruel and unafraid of everything.

PIRATE SONG

PIRATES: WE'RE MEAN
            SO VERY MEAN
            WE KICK DOGS AND CATS
            AND TAKE CANDY FROM BABIES
            WE LIKE TO EAT GNATS
            AND WE THINK WE HAVE RABIES
            WE LOVE IT AND THAT'S WHY
            THERE'S NO IF'S OR MAYBE'S
            WE'RE OBSCENELY MEAN.

CLARISSA: There was only one thing in the whole world that they
            feared: *(PIRATES all listen to hear what it's going to*

10

be.) their captain, Clarissa.

(PIRATES lift her up and put patch on her eye and knife in her hand.)

CLARISSA'S PIRATES: The Mean!

PIRATE SONG

PIRATES and CLARISSA: WE'RE MEAN
SO VERY MEAN
WE KICK DOGS AND CATS
AND TAKE CANDY FROM BABIES
WE LIKE TO EAT GNATS
AND WE THINK WE HAVE RABIES
WE LOVE IT AND THAT'S WHY
THERE'S NO IF'S OR MAYBE'S
WE'RE OBSCENELY MEAN.

CLARISSA: To work you lazy, no good bums! The sky looks ominous. We'll see trouble before this day is done.

CLARISSA'S PIRATES: And she was right.

FIRST PIRATE: Look, Captain, another pirate ship looms on the horizon!

SECOND PIRATE: That's the Dark Demon!

CLARISSA'S PIRATES: Oh no!

FIRST PIRATE: That'll be Dirty Dan's Dark Demon. He's the ugliest pirate in the world!

PIRATES: We're lost!

CLARISSA: You chickens! Have you forgotten? You're sailing with Clarissa the Mean!

PIRATE SONG

PIRATES and CLARISSA: WE'RE MEAN
SO VERY MEAN
WE KICK DOGS AND CATS
AND TAKE CANDY FROM BABIES
WE LIKE TO EAT GNATS
AND WE THINK WE HAVE RABIES
WE LOVE IT AND THAT'S WHY
THERE'S NO IF'S OR MAYBE'S
WE'RE OBSCENELY MEAN.

CLARISSA: I'll make ol' peg leg rue the day he came into my part of the seven seas. All hands man your stations.

DIRTY DAN: *(Enters.)* The Dark Demon sailed into view with Dirty Dan, the ugliest pirate in the world, surrounded by the most grotesque band of sailors who ever lived. The two ships faced off for the greatest sea battle of the century.

CLARISSA: Ahoy there, Dark Demon. You haven't a chance, Dirty. You'd better surrender now before we sink your ship.

DIRTY DAN: Never, Mean! We'll fight you to the death.

CLARISSA: Oh, yeah?

DIRTY DAN: Yeah! Ready the cannons, mates!

CLARISSA'S PIRATES: Oh, no! The cannons!

CLARISSA: We have cannons, too, you idiots.

CLARISSA'S PIRATES: Oh, good.

CLARISSA: Man your stations.

DIRTY DAN: Fire the cannons!

(PIRATES light cannons; do sound sssssssssss-boom! CLARISSA'S PIRATES duck each ball.)

CLARISSA: Fire back, you cowards!

(CLARISSA'S PIRATES light and fire cannons. DIRTY DAN'S duck the first two. THEY scatter when hit by the third.)

ONE OF CLARISSA'S PIRATES: A direct hit, Captain.

CLARISSA: Good work. Now, bring us along side - - we're going to board.

DIRTY DAN: To arms, men! Ready your swords and knives.

CLARISSA: Swords and knives?! You, Scum! We'll show you we're better than that. Right, men?!

CLARISSA'S PIRATES: Right! *(THEY pull axes, lances, chains, etc. out of the closet.)*

CLARISSA: No, you lily-livered nothings! We'll fight them bare-handed!

CLARISSA'S PIRATES: Bare-handed?

DIRTY DAN: So, it's to be hand-to-hand combat, eh?

CLARISSA: You heard me right.

DIRTY DAN: I'll say this for you, Mean, you sure are brave. But, you're going to regret this. Get 'em, Men!

CLARISSA: Into the fray, you bums. *(ALL PIRATES fight.)* Take that, Dirty. *(SHE knocks him out.)* Push him overboard. *(DIRTY swims away.)* Ah, ha! We've won. *(To remaining PIRATE or PIRATES.)* And now for you. *(CLARISSA'S PIRATES advance on DIRTY DAN'S*

PIRATES as MOM enters.)

MOM:	How's the cleaning going, Clarissa?

(PIRATES hide. CLARISSA looks at room - - it is a mess.)

CLARISSA:	Fine, Mom. I'm nearly finished. *(Stuffs her pillow into can.)* The can's half full.

MOM:	That's good. Grandma can sleep in your room. Won't that be nice? *(Sniffs air.)* She'll be here tomorrow, Clarissa.

CLARISSA:	I know. But, I don't think Grandma likes us.

MOM:	Of course, she likes us. She's always liked us *(Sniff.)* Why do you think she doesn't like us? *(Sniff.)*

CLARISSA:	Because she hasn't come to see us since I was a little kid.

MOM:	Oh, that. She retired. Retired people travel in large groups moving very slowly. She does write us, you know.

(MOM sneaks something off the floor into the can. CLARISSA takes it out.)

MOM:	Don't stay up too late, Dear.

CLARISSA:	I won't.

MOM:	If you need help . . . ?

CLARISSA:	No. I'll do it, Mom.

(MOM goes to exit and comes back. PIRATES may come out and have to rehide.)

14

MOM:	Clarissa?
CLARISSA:	Yes, Mom.
MOM:	If you can't find the smell, I'll have to do it myself.
CLARISSA:	No! I'll find it!
MOM:	I'm sure you'll do your best. *(MOM exits.)*
CLARISSA:	*(To hiding PIRATES.)* We'll let you go this time - - but take your junk with you. *(PIRATES exit with some junk.)* Take that, too. *(CLARISSA sifts through junk; SHE doesn't know where to start.)*
CLARISSA:	It's too late. I can't do it now; I'm tired. My feet are tired, my hands are tired, my back is tired, my head is tired . . . *(CLARISSA curls up on her bed and goes to sleep. Magical sound comes from closet as MOM enters. Then there are sounds of the sea. MOM is dressed as a marathon swimmer. SHE lies on stool or in some way indicates she is swimming. Sounds of waves and storm.)*
MOM:	This is it. I've had it. The waves are too high. The storm is getting worse. I don't think I can make it, Dad. *(DAD enters from closet. He is her trainer. HE mimes being in a small boat.)*
DAD:	Sure you can, Mom. You have to. You said you would. Here, eat this orange.
MOM:	It's not peeled.
DAD:	Oh. Let me do that. Keep swimming, Mom.

MOM:	You're supposed to look out for sharks and sting-rays and men-of-war, not peel oranges.
DAD:	I am looking. You know, you're getting grouchy, Mom.
MOM:	I know. Maybe this is too much to ask of myself. After all, nobody else has swum non-stop from Japan to Australia. Why did I think I could be the first to make it? Why must I always ask so much of myself?
DAD:	You're sinking, Mom. I think you'd better use your feet, too.
MOM:	Are you listening to me?
DAD:	Of course I am. I'm also looking for sharks, sting-rays and men-of-war and I'm peeling an orange.
MOM:	Maybe you could swim with me, Dad. That would be nice.
DAD:	But, Mom, you're the greatest swimmer in the world. I couldn't keep up with you.
MOM:	That's true. I can't go on. I simply can't go on! *(But she does.)* Wait . . . What's that, Dad?
DAD:	Oh, no. I thought you'd be spared this, Mom.
MOM:	Is it a shark, Dad?
DAD:	Worse than that - - it's Clarissa's closet!
MOM:	But, I can't even walk through that , let alone swim.
DAD:	Don't you see, Mom, it doesn't matter - - the smell will kill up both anyway. Oh, we tried to tell her, but she won't listen.

MOM: And now it's too late.

DAD: No, wait, Mom. There's someone out there - - someone
                is coming to help us. It's . . . *(HE's looking through
                binoculars.)* it's Grandma! Here we are, Grandma!

MOM: No! Go back, Grandma. Don't breathe in!

DAD: Of course. You're right, Mom. No use us all dying.

                (BOTH shout for Grandma to stay back.)

DAD: She can't hear us - - we're all lost! Good-bye, Grandma
                . . . Good-bye, Mom.

MOM: If only Clarissa had listened . . . *(MOM and DAD are
                'washed' offstage to exit.)*

CLARISSA: No! Don't drown! *(Sitting up suddenly.)* Don't drown!
                I'll do it! I'll listen! *(Realizing it was only a dream.)* Only
                a dream. Get control of yourself, Clarissa, you're really
                getting weird. *(SHE lies down and chuckles to herself
                but it dies out. SHE sits up.)* All right, all right. Maybe it
                does smell like something in here. I could look for it, I
                guess. *(To closet.)* Don't look at me like that - - I have
                to. My Grandma is old and she doesn't like smells.
                (SHE reluctantly takes something out.) Look at this. I
                use this every day. And this . . . I need this. *(SHE
                brings things out and rejects throwing them away.)* No .
                . . No . . . *(SHE throws herself into the search and
                comes out with a feather. SHE smells it and puts it in
                the can. She needs more.)* This isn't easy. Look at this
                thing. I don't remember what it does. I think I made it
                myself. It could be a rocket . . . or a turtle . . . maybe it
                was a gift for my Mom. I better keep it. *(Back into
                closet.)* Ow! I think I've found something. *(SHE
                struggles with a tree branch.)* It's part of my birthday
                tree. I remember the day Dad told me I owned a tree. I
                was only four.

(DAD enters from closet.)

DAD: You see this tree, Clarissa?

CLARISSA: Yes, Dad. I do.

DAD: It's your tree. I planted it here the day you were born.

CLARISSA: It's a nice tree, Dad. But, it's pretty big for a four year
            old.

DAD: Oh, it's older than you are, Clarissa. It was ten years old
            when I put it here. But, I planted it for you. So that you
            would have a big beautiful tree to play in when you grew
            up. It's your birthday tree.

CLARISSA: My birthday tree. I'll buy it a present next year.

DAD: And when you're older we'll build a tree house.

CLARISSA: A tree house! Can we build it now, Dad?

DAD: Hmmmm. Given the size of this tree, it'd have to be a
            pretty small tree house. No. We'll build it when the tree
            is ready.

CLARISSA: All right, Dad.

DAD: I know. You can design it, Clarissa. That's a good
            hobby and it could take years.

CLARISSA: Ok. How will I do that?

DAD: I'll go think about it. Thinking is a good hobby, too.
            (DAD exits into closet.)

CLARISSA: It was my tree. I was going to give it a hummingbird
            feeder and some vitamins for its birthday. But, then . . .
            (DAD enters.)

18

DAD: Clarissa?

CLARISSA: Yes, Dad?

DAD: We have to move, Clarissa. I'm sorry. You'll have to leave your tree.

CLARISSA: Oh no. How will it live if I'm not here? It'll get lonely.

DAD: The people who move here will look after it. In fact, they'll probably have a little girl or boy who will love it as much as you do.

CLARISSA: Are you going to let those kids and their Dad build my tree house in it?

DAD: Clarissa. Even if you live in a different place, I planted this tree for you. It's your birthday tree and you can come back and visit it and watch it grow older and taller - - just like you. Why don't you take a little piece of it to keep you company. Collecting memories is a very good hobby. *(DAD exits.)*

(SHE takes cutting off of the tree and puts the rest of the tree in the can.)

CLARISSA: Good-bye, tree. I'll remember you're mine. And I'll come back to see you - - maybe when I have a car. I can't do any more. I don't care if it stinks in here. I'm not old - - I like it like this. *(SHE puts blanket, shoes, hat and finally Peter's bowling ball into the can.)* Now it's full.

(PETER enters. He's in pajamas.)

PETER: What are you doing, Clarissa?

CLARISSA: *(Hiding can.)* Peter! I never said you could come in my room.

PETER:	You woke me up. What are you doing up in the middle of the night?
CLARISSA:	I've got a right to be up in my room if I want to.
PETER:	Not if you wake me up. I don't like to be awake in the middle of the night.
CLARISSA:	Why? Are you scared?
PETER:	Of course not. I am never afraid. But, I do like to get a good night's sleep.
CLARISSA:	Never?
PETER:	Never what?
CLARISSA:	Never afraid.
PETER:	That's right.
CLARISSA:	Do you want to hear a story I wrote? *(SHE looks for a story.)*
PETER:	Now? In the middle of the night?
CLARISSA:	Sure. I think it's a great story. *(Finds story.)* Are you ready?
PETER:	No, I'm not ready. It's the middle of the night - - ordinary people sleep during the night and I can't stay in here - - it stinks. I'm going back to bed.
CLARISSA:	*(Holds HIM.)* Just listen to this. You'll like it.
PETER:	Clarissa! Let me go.
CLARISSA:	See? You are scared.

PETER: This better be quick.

CLARISSA: *(Reading. Sounds come from closet and strange things happen in the room - - perhaps the clothes come alive - - as Clarissa tells the story.)* 'The night was dark and gloomy. And she was alone . . .

PETER: I'm not going to listen to this.

CLARISSA: 'I'm not alone,' she thought wildly. The cold and clammy room was filled with strange sighs and whispering voices. *(Whispers.)* 'The walls are moving! I knew I wasn't alone.' *(Low moan.)* What was that? I'll never make it,' she sobbed. The ticking of the clock was relentless. Chills ran up her spine as the walls moved closer and closer. She felt trapped. 'This house is evil, evil, evil,' she cried. They told me it would win and I would lose. But, I didn't listen. Now, look at me! *(Scream.)* 'What was that? I don't know who - - or what - - you are!' she said. And still the walls moved closer and closer. There was no way out . . . she was going to be smashed, and she knew it. Just then a strange sight appeared before her. *(An eye appears.)* It was one large eye. It spoke.

PETER: How can an eye speak?

(Sound stop.)

CLARISSA: Shut up, Peter. Just listen.

PETER: I was only wondering how . . .

CLARISSA: The eye spoke: *(Sounds again.)* 'You'll never escape this evil, evil house. You're going to get smashed to death.' And then it disappeared into thin air. *(EYE disappears.)* The walls were very close now and the clock kept ticking. Ghostly voices seemed to be laughing at her; ghostly sounds filled the room - - or what

21

was left of it. 'I'll never make it!,' she cried!

PETER:　　　Is she going to make it?

CLARISSA:　　You'll have to listen to find out.

PETER:　　　I don't trust you, Clarissa.

CLARISSA:　　Where was I? Oh . . . *(Building.)* . . . the walls kept
inching in, the clock kept ticking, the ghostly voices kept
laughing, the screams and moans bounced off the close
walls. The small room was filled with fear, horror, terror,
and trembling. It looked like it was the end of her!!!

PETER:　　　Stop! ! *(HE's scared.)*

CLARISSA:　　Why? ! ! *(SHE's scared.)*

PETER:　　　*(In a small voice.)* I want to go to sleep now.

CLARISSA:　　Wait. You have to hear the ending.

PETER:　　　No. I don't want to.

CLARISSA:　　*(Holding on to HIM.)* 'It looked like she was going to be
crushed *(SHE makes a decision.)* when suddenly, with
strength she never knew she had, she began to push
back the walls . . . and she was saved!'

　　　　　　　(Sounds stop.)

PETER:　　　She was saved?

CLARISSA:　　Yes. She was saved.

PETER:　　　She was saved? She was saved! Thank you, Clarissa.

CLARISSA:　　You're welcome, Peter. I was right - - this is a great
story. Maybe I better work on the ending.

22

PETER: I think I'll go back to bed now. Oh, no! Look! *(Looking at clock.)*

CLARISSA: What's wrong?

PETER: It's morning already. It's time to get up.

CLARISSA: So?

PETER: So? I didn't get a good night's sleep. Grandma is coming today. It's bad enough that this room stinks and now this. Look at my eyes - - I can hardly see, I'm so tired. And look at this room. You can't write now - - you've got to clean up this mess. Old people cannot stand messes. I don't think this is going to be a very good day. *(HE exits.)*

CLARISSA: 'Death on the High Seas:' Chapter 87 *(PIRATES are heard singing their song from closet.)* 'Clarissa meets the Sea Creature.'

    (SEA CREATURE is half-way out of closet as DAD enters. SEA CREATURE backs in.)

DAD: Clarissa?

CLARISSA: Yes, Dad?

DAD: How's the cleaning going?

CLARISSA: Oh . . . I filled the can, Dad.

DAD: Fine. *(Sniffs the air - - still smells.)* Would you like me to empty it for you?

CLARISSA: No thanks, Dad. I'll do it.

DAD: Fine. We were planning on letting Grandma sleep in here, Clarissa.

CLARISSA:	I know. Dad?
	(DAD is trying to get a peak into the closet.)
DAD:	*(Feeling caught.)* Yes, what?
CLARISSA:	What do very old people do for fun?
DAD:	I don't know - - maybe they read the newspaper.
CLARISSA:	That's fun?
DAD:	Oh, sure. Reading the newspaper is lots of fun if you're very old. Are you sure you don't need any help?
CLARISSA:	I'm sure, Dad.
DAD:	Fine. Keep up the good work, Clarissa.
CLARISSA:	I will. *(DAD exits.)* Reading the newspaper? I'm never going to get old. *(PETER enters with fish bowl.)*
	I didn't say you could come in, Peter. Don't say anything. I'm busy. *(Pause.)* Why are you carrying your fish bowl? *(PETER wordlessly holds it out.)* Where's Spot? *(PETER indicates HIS fish, SPOT is dead.)* Dead?
PETER:	Then SHE flushed him down the toilet.
CLARISSA:	Oh. She didn't know it was Spot.
PETER:	What will happen to him? It must be awful down there.
CLARISSA:	No. Dead fish like to be flushed down the toilet.
PETER:	How could they? You're just saying that to make me feel better.

CLARISSA:	But, lots of Moms and Dads flush dead fish down the toilet. They must be sending them somewhere.
PETER:	Where do they go down there?
CLARISSA:	*(SHE gets an idea.)* Fish Heaven.
PETER:	In the toilet?
CLARISSA:	No, but a fish angel will find him.
PETER:	Come on, Clarissa. There are fish angels?
CLARISSA:	There must be. Big, beautiful fish with small golden wings. *(FISH ANGEL enters.)* One of them will find Spot.
PETER:	How could a big, beautiful fish angel find Spot in the toilet?
CLARISSA:	*(FISH ANGEL does action.)* He'll dive down into the pipes and swim and swim and swim faster than speed itself until he reaches Spot. Then he'll scoop Spot up and swim even faster until he reaches the ocean where he'll skim along the bottom far out into the very middle. Then that angel will shoot up into the sky carrying Spot with him. And he'll fly way, way, way out there, to another ocean called fish heaven. And there Spot will become a fish angel, too.

(FISH ANGEL begins song. Other FISH ANGELS enter and sing chorus.)

FISH HEAVEN

FISH ANGEL: MY STORY'S QUITE BIZARRE
BUT FRANKLY SO AM I
THE TALE I TELL IS ALL ABOUT YOUR

FISH ANGEL: FISH WHEN THEY DIE
THAT PET WHO'S ALWAYS WET
HAS MY SOLEMN GUARANTEE
THAT HE HAS GOT A PEACEFUL SPOT
FOR ALL ETERNITY
IT'S CALLED FISH HEAVEN

ANGELETTES: THAT'S WHERE FISH GO WHEN
THEY DIE YI-YI-YI

FISH ANGEL: FISH HEAVEN

ANGELETTES: THAT'S THE FISH BOWL
IN THE SKY YI-YI-YI
(OOH, OOH, WAH)

FISH ANGEL: WITH ONE FIN IN THE GRAVE
I KNOW A FISH CAN'T FEEL MUCH BLUER
WHEN HE RIDES THAT FINAL WAVE
IT'S DOWN THE TOILET TO THE SEWER.
BUT DON'T FRET

ANGELETTES: GET READY, GET SET

FISH ANGEL: YOU'LL MAKE IT YET

ANGELETTES: IT'S REALLY NO SWEAT

FISH ANGEL: TO FISH HEAVEN

ANGELETTES: LA, DA, DA, DA
LA, DA, DA, DA

FISH ANGEL: I'LL ALWAYS BE THERE
WHEN SOMEONE FLUSHES
AS I HURRY TO SEARCH EACH LITTLE DRAIN
I'LL BE ANYWHERE
THE SEWER PIPE GUSHES
TO SCURRY FOR PERCH IN A LURCH

FISH ANGEL: OR SALMON IN PAIN
YOU MIGHT THINK THAT
IT'S ODD, THE THINGS I SAY NOW.
I TELL EACH POOR, LIFELESS COD
HE'LL BE OK.
YEA, THOUGH YOU SWIM THROUGH
THE FISH BOWL OF THE SHADOW OF DEATH
YOU KNOW THAT I CARE
AND YOU KNOW I'LL BE THERE
'WHEN YOU SIP YOUR LAST BREATH
COME TO FISH HEAVEN

ANGELETTES: THAT'S WHERE FISH GO WHEN THEY
DIE YI-YI-YI

FISH ANGEL: FISH HEAVEN

ANGELETTES: THAT'S THE FISH BOWL
IN THE SKY YI-YI-YI
(OOH, OOH, WAH)

FISH ANGEL: WITH ONE FIN IN THE GRAVE
I KNOW A FISH CAN'T FEEL MUCH BLUER
WHEN HE RIDES THAT FINAL WAVE
IT'S DOWN THE TOILET TO THE SEWER
BUT DON'T FRET

ANGELETTES: GET READY, GET SET

FISH ANGEL: YOU'LL MAKE IT YET

ANGELETTES: IT'S REALLY NO SWEAT

FISH ANGEL: TO FISH HEAVEN.

EACH DEAD LITTLE TROUT
AND PERISHED GOLDFISH
AND EACH SAD LITTLE SHAD
AND PASSED-AWAY CARP

FISH ANGEL: ALL LISTEN'D WITH CARE
              TO WHAT I TOLD FISH
              AND NOW THEY'RE LAYING ON CLOUDS
              AND PLAYING A HARP
              SO SICKLY OLD FLOUNDER
              DON'T YOU FEAR NOW
              AND THEN WHEN IT'S ALL DONE
              YOU GIVE A CHEER
              AFTER THE FINAL TIDE EBBS
              AND YOU'RE ON YOUR LAST FINS
              DON'T YOU DESPAIR
              I WILL MAKE YOU AWARE
              THAT'S WHEN NEW LIFE BEGINS
              COME TO FISH HEAVEN

ANGELETTES: THAT'S WHERE FISH GO WHEN THEY
              DIE YI-YI-YI

FISH ANGEL: FISH HEAVEN

ANGELETTES: THAT'S THE FISH BOWL IN THE
              SKY-YI-YI-YI

FISH ANGEL: WITH ONE FIN IN THE GRAVE
              I KNOW A FISH CAN'T FEEL MUCH BLUER
              WHEN HE RIDES THAT FINAL WAVE
              IT'S DOWN THE TOILET TO THE SEWER
              BUT DON'T FRET?

ANGELETTES: GET READY, GET SET

FISH ANGEL: YOU'LL MAKE IT YET

ANGELETTES: IT'S REALLY NO SWEAT

FISH ANGEL: TO FISH HEAVEN, OOH

ANGELETTES: HEAVEN
              SAILING, SAILING UP TO FISH HEAVEN
              NOW

(All FISH ANGELS exit.)

CLARISSA: Now, don't you feel better?

PETER: No. But, thanks anyway.

CLARISSA: Here, Peter, let me read you a story. It's all about pirates and it's very good.

PETER: No.

CLARISSA: You can be the Captain. *(SHE dresses him as a Pirate.)*

PETER: I don't really like your stories, Clarissa.

(As THEY speak, PIRATES enter singing MEAN SONG: OH, HE'S MEAN, SO VERY MEAN . . .)

CLARISSA: You'll like this one. You get to be real mean in it.

PETER: But, I'm not a mean person.

CLARISSA: You have to be mean or they won't obey you. *(PIRATES surround PETER and growl at HIM.)* Here, he is men. Peter the Pirate. *(PIRATES pick him up and chant 'He's #1.')* Go on, Peter.

PETER: What do I say?

CLARISSA: Tell them they won't eat for a week.

PETER: You won't eat for a week. *(PIRATES grumble and cower.)*

CLARISSA: Tell them they have to scrub the deck.

PETER: Scrub the deck.

CLARISSA: Fix the sails.

PETER: You - - fix the sails.

CLARISSA: And shine your shoes.

PETER: Shine my shoes. You have to do it. *(PIRATES really grumble at this indignity but they shine his shoes.)*

CLARISSA: Good, Peter. Now tell them they'll do bloody battle every day and fight to the death whenever you say.

PETER: You'll fight to the death every day! *(SONG: BECAUSE I'M MEAN, SO VERY MEAN. PIRATES have a conference as PETER sings.)* Why are you standing there, you cowards? Get to work! You lily-livered, no good, dumb chicken bums!

              (PIRATES pick PETER up, set up a plank and carry him to it.)

PETER: What are you doing? I didn't say you could do this. We have battles to fight.

ONE PIRATE: Peter the Pirate?

PETER: Yes?

SECOND PIRATE: We've decided to make you walk the plank.

PETER: What?

PIRATES: Yeah, the plank!

PETER: You can't do that.

ONE PIRATE: Yes, we can.

PETER: But I'm the captain.

SECOND PIRATE: So what. This is mutiny!

PIRATES: Hooray! Mutiny!

PETER: Mutiny? Why?

ONE PIRATE: Because you're so mean.

PETER: But, Clarissa said I was supposed to be mean.

SECOND PIRATE: Yeah, well, you're too mean. Push him off!

PETER: No! Wait!

PIRATES: Push him . . . push him . . .

PETER: Clarissa! Stop them! Help me!

CLARISSA: Don't worry, Peter. I'll save you. *(SHE fights PIRATES. Aside to PETER.)* Great story, isn't it?

PETER: *(Fighting PIRATES.)* Ouch! I don't like your stories, Clarissa. Wait. Stop, Clarissa. I hear something. Shhh. *(ALL stop.)*

CLARISSA: What is it?

PETER: I heard something.

CLARISSA: What do you hear?

PETER: Voices.

               (EVERYONE listens. Voices are heard.)

CLARISSA: Who's voices are they?

PETER: I bet it's Grandma. She's here!

CLARISSA: Oh. *(As in: Is that all. SHE goes back to fighting but PIRATES are worried like PETER.)*

PETER:	NO! Stop! *(PIRATES stop.)* Look at this mess. You didn't clean it up at all.
CLARISSA:	I did so.
PETER:	No you didn't. It's worse than ever. Grandma can't see this. It's embarrassing. *(PIRATES start to exit, embarrassed.)*
CLARISSA:	This is how it always looks. We like it like this, don't we? *(SHE looks at PIRATES who ALL shake heads sadly.)*
PETER:	That's it. I've got to go fix a place for Grandma in my room.
CLARISSA:	But Mom and Dad said Grandma was going to sleep with me.
PETER:	She can't stay in here - - it's horrible.
CLARISSA:	Watch it, Peter.
PETER:	It's awful. *(CLOSET reacts.)* Grandmas are old and weak. Rotten smells can kill them. And this room is rotten.
CLARISSA:	You better leave, Peter.
PETER:	There is something in there that stinks *(Points to CLOSET which growls back.)*
CLARISSA:	Peter . . .
PETER:	I would throw everything out of that closet, scrub the walls and put up an air freshener. *(CLOSET gasps.)*
CLARISSA:	Get out of my room, Peter. Now. *(Pushing him out.)*
PETER:	Mom and Dad won't let Grandma stay in here.

CLARISSA: *(Pushing.)* I don't care. I don't care if Grandma doesn't like me or my room.

PETER: You don't care if Grandma gets sick . . .

CLARISSA: Ok, I don't care!

PETER: Clarissa! You're supposed to love your Grandma.

CLARISSA: Get out.

             (SHE succeeds in pushing PETER out. HE exits.)

             I didn't ask her to come. *(Sadly surveys the mess.)* All this trouble for some old grandma who doesn't like messes and smells and reads the newspaper all day. She wouldn't like me.

CLARISSA: Little John?

             (LITTLE JOHN appears.)

LITTLE JOHN: Yes, Robin?

CLARISSA: Where's my bow and arrows?

LITTLE JOHN: *(Looking at the mess.)* Gee, Robin, I don't know. You haven't used them in a long time.

CLARISSA: Well, help me find them.

LITTLE JOHN: Oh, certainly. Merry men! *(MERRY MEN appear.)* Find Robin's bow and arrows. *(To CLARISSA)* We'll have them for you in a minute, Robin. Look over there, Men. Find anything? *(ONE MERRY MEN looking through junk in room shakes head.)* We're looking, Robin. It's not easy to find something in all this - - you know.

CLARISSA: I know.

33

A MERRY MAN: Ah. Look at this.

LITTLE JOHN: What's that?

A MERRY MAN: I don't know.

CLARISSA: Those are letters - - from my Grandma.

LITTLE JOHN: Oh, so they are.

CLARISSA: She always writes to me.

LITTLE JOHN: All those letters. She must like you, Robin.

CLARISSA: *(Not convinced.)* I suppose so.

LITTLE JOHN: Right. These aren't what we're looking for. *(HE throws them into can.)* Keep looking, Men. Don't despair, Robin. The bow and arrows are bound to be somewhere in this- - ah . . . you know.

A MERRY MAN: Ah. What's this?

CLARISSA: That was a gift - - from my Grandma.

LITTLE JOHN: Nice. Very nice. *(HE's not sure what it is.)*

CLARISSA: It's a hat.

LITTLE JOHN: So it is. But, it's not your bow and arrows. And that's what you want - - isn't it?

CLARISSA: I guess so.

LITTLE JOHN: *(HE throws gift into can.)* Keep looking, Men.

A MERRY MAN: How about this?

LITTLE JOHN: That's just a photo. Who cares about that?

CLARISSA: I do. That's my Grandma holding me when I was a baby.

ALL: Ahhhh.

LITTLE JOHN: But Robin, we don't need this - - we need your bow and arrows. *(HE goes to throw photo into can.)*

CLARISSA: Wait. *(SHE takes things out of can.)* Give me that. She is my only Grandma. *(ALL react.)* And she likes me a lot. *(ALL agree.)* Maybe I'll like her, too. *(ALL "Maybe")* The least I could do for her would be to clean up my room for her visit. *(ALL agree.)* And find the smell! *(ALL cheer.)* Oh, I'll do it- - but, I've got to do this fast.

FIND THE SMELL / FOR GRANDMA

CLOSET VOICES: OOH, OOH

CLARISSA: FIND THE SMELL

MERRY MEN: FIND THE SMELL

CLARISSA: 'CAUSE GRANDMA'S ON HER WAY UP HERE

MERRY MEN: 'CAUSE GRANDMA'S ON HER WAY HERE

CLARISSA: FIND THE SMELL

MERRY MEN: FIND THE SMELL

CLARISSA: 'CAUSE GRANDMA'S GONNA STAY UP HERE

MERRY MEN: 'CAUSE GRANDMA'S GONNA STAY HERE

CLARISSA: GET THE THINGS INSIDE THE CLOSET OUT
IF SOMETHING STINKS WE SIMPLY TOSS IT OUT
FOR GRANDMA
FIND THE SMELL

MERRY MEN: FIND THE SMELL

CLARISSA: OR SHE COULD PASS AWAY IN HERE

MERRY MAN 1: THIS BUNDLE OF CLOTHING UNFOLDED

CLARISSA: THAT'S THE SUIT THAT I WEAR WHEN I SWIM

MERRY MAN 1: THIS TOWEL IS TOTALLY MOLDED

CLARISSA: I USED IT LAST MONTH IN THE GYM

MERRY MAN 2: WHATEVER YOU HAD IN THIS LUNCH BOX
              HAS SLOWLY BEGUN TO DECAY

CLARISSA: IT WAS PEANUT BUTTER AND JELLY

MERRY MAN 2: IT'S UTTERLY SMELLY

CLARISSA: SO THROW IT AWAY

CLARISSA: *(Spoken under music.)* Just an old sandwich and a
              moldy towel? This is going to be easier than I thought.

MERRY MAN 3: What's this?

CLARISSA: That's my project from last year's Science Fair at school.
              It was all about vinegar and sulfur and stuff like that. I
              won fifth prize. See?

MERRY MAN 3: THE RIBBON YOU GOT MUST HAVE THRILLED
              YOU
              BUT YOUR VINEGAR JAR HAS A LEAK

MERRY MAN 2: *(Under.)* FIND THE SMELL *(Repeated.)*

MERRY MAN 3: THE PAPERS ARE COVERED WITH MILDEW
              THE SULFUR HAS STARTED TO REEK

CLARISSA: IT MIGHT BE A CHEMICAL BREAKTHROUGH
TO HELP THE SURVIVAL OF MAN

MERRY MAN 3: IT'S GROWING WITH ROT AND IT'S GOING TO POT
AND I'M THROWING IT INTO THE CAN

CLARISSA: Stop. How can you throw away something so
important? You may be standing in the way of science.

LITTLE JOHN: FOR GRANDMA
WE MUST PICK UP THIS MESS
FOR GRANDMA
COULD GET SICK FROM THE SMELL
POOR GRANDMA'S
NO SPRING CHICKEN SO UNLESS
YOU CLEAR THE SMELL OUT FASTER
YOU CLEARLY SPELL DISASTER
FOR GRANDMA

CLARISSA: FOR GRANDMA
TAKE THAT ROTTEN DEBRIS
FOR GRANDMA
THROW THE LOT IN THE CAN
THAT OLD GREY MARE AIN'T WHAT SHE USED TO
BE

MERRY MEN: SO GO TO WORK OR SOON YOU'LL
BE GOING TO THE FUN'RAL
FOR GRANDMA

MERRY MAN 1: IF ONLY SOMEONE WHO WAS SMART
WENT OUT TO CALL THE HEALTH DEPARTMENT
OUT
WHEN ALL OF THIS MESS FIRST BEGAN

MERRY MAN 2: 'CAUSE WITH YOUR ROOM THE WAY IT IS
IT'S GONNA RUIN GRANDMA'S VISIT

ALL: SO WE BETTER KEEP FILLING THE CAN

MERRY MEN: *(Under.)* OOH, OOH

CLARISSA: MY GRANDMA
MAY BE WEARY AND WEAK
AND GRANDMA
MAY NOT HEAR WHEN WE SPEAK

ALL: BUT GRANDMA IS OUR DEAREST OLD ANTIQUE
IT'S NICE IF YOU CAN SHARE ROOMS
WITH PRICELESS FAMILY HEIRLOOMS
LIKE GRANDMA

CLARISSA: WE WENT TO THE BEACH ON VACATION
AND THIS WAS MY FAVORITE SHELL

MERRY MAN 3: YOU FORGOT TO REMOVE THE CRUSTACEAN
(SO) HE DIED AND HE'S STARTING TO SMELL

CLARISSA: I MADE THIS AT SCHOOL IN MY ART CLASS
IT USED TO BE PAPIER MACHE

MERRY MAN 3: WELL I DON'T KNOW ART
BUT I KNOW WHAT I LIKE
AND I'D LIKE YOU TO THROW IT AWAY

MERRY MEN: *(Under)* FIND THE SMELL
'CAUSE GRANDMA'S ON HER WAY UP HERE
FIND THE SMELL
'CAUSE GRANDMA'S GOING TO STAY UP HERE

CLARISSA: ELIMINATE STENCH OR BEWARE THE DISMAY
OF WOMEN WITH DENTURES AND HAIR THAT IS
GREY
POOR GRANDMA
I CAN BE RUTHLESS AND DO WHAT I MUST
'CAUSE SHE CAN BE TOOTHLESS
AND STILL BITE THE DUST
WHEN WE FINALLY GET THE SMELL FROM THAT
THEN IT'S TIME TO SET THE WELCOME MAT

ALL: FOR GRANDMA

MERRY MEN: *(Under.)* FIND THE SMELL
              OR SHE COULD PASS AWAY

CLARISSA: SHE CAN BE WRINKLY STILL I DON'T CARE
              BREATHING THE STINK'LL BE TOO MUCH TO BEAR
              SHE'LL PASS AWAY

MERRY MAN 1: What's this?

CLARISSA: THAT'S A PRESENT I MADE FOR MY MOTHER

MERRY MAN 1: IT'S A BEAUTIFUL JAPANESE FAN

CLARISSA: WELL SOMEDAY I'LL MAKE HER ANOTHER
              'CAUSE NOW IT GOES INTO THE CAN

MERRY MAN 2: What are these?

CLARISSA: THOSE PAPERS ARE THINGS THAT I'VE WRITTEN
              SOME STORIES, A POEM, A PLAY

MERRY MEN 2: YOU CAN SAVE THEM I THINK
              BECAUSE THEY DO NOT STINK

CLARISSA: WELL, THANK YOU
              BUT THROW THEM AWAY

MERRY MAN 1: What about this?

CLARISSA: Throw it away!

MERRY MEN: *(One after another)* What about this?

CLARISSA: THROW IT ALL AWAY

MERRY MEN: THROW IT AWAY, THROW IT AWAY, THROW IT
              AWAY

CLARISSA: Everything goes!

ALL: FOR GRANDMA

              (PETER enters.)

PETER: Clarissa! They're coming up the stairs. Wow you did it.
              I don't believe it.

DAD: *(Off stage.)* Do you need help, Grandma?

PETER: I'll help her. Grandmas always need help climbing
              stairs.

              *(PETER exits. PETER screams. GRANDMA enters
              carrying PETER on her back. GRANDMA is very
              eccentric looking - - kind of a successful, world traveled
              bag lady.)*

MOM AND DAD: Peter!

CLARISSA: Grandma? !

GRANDMA: I think he fainted.

PETER: Is that our Grandma?

MOM AND DAD: Of course.

CLARISSA: Wow.

              (PETER faints again.)

GRANDMA: It must be the excitement. I feel a bit flushed myself.
              And I'm in the best of health.

CLARISSA: You don't look old and weak. You look wonderful.

GRANDMA: I know. I've been working out and traveling. Traveling is a very good hobby. But, look at you, Clarissa. You're all grown up. *(Sniffs air.)* Hmmm. Interesting smell *(ALL react.)* I can't place it. *(Sniff, sniff.)* It reminds me of a home I once owned - - in the country. *(Sniff.)* Hmmmm. Nice.

PETER: Does that mean you like the way it smells in here?

GRANDMA: Oh, yes. I always loved the country. And the world is a smelly place, Peter.

CLARISSA: I love you, Grandma.

GRANDMA: And I love you, Clarissa. And you, too, Peter.

PETER: I don't feel very good.

GRANDMA: Oh? You should get more exercise.

CLARISSA: Tell us about your adventures, Grandma. Did you get attacked by robbers? Were you ever in real danger? Did you see any pirates?

PETER: How could she see any pirates? Grandmas always travel with tour guides on buses. There are no pirates on buses.

GRANDMA: Actually, I always travel alone, it's more exciting that way *(To Clarissa)* and dangerous.

CLARISSA: Wow.

PETER: But, buses aren't dangerous . . .

GRANDMA: I travel by sea. I'm reminded of a stormy night off the Barbary Coast. The waves were so high I thought we would all be lost. Up and down we went. Up and down. The water washed over the deck while we all clung to the rails, our hands freezing and bloody with the effort.

GRANDMA: *(SHE shouts at the Captain.)* "Are we gonners, Captain?" I shouted above the roar of the storm. He didn't answer, for at that very moment a giant wave washed over our little vessel and carried the Captain and several passengers out into the merciless depths. 'Oh, you cruel, cruel sea," I cried into the night.

(MOM and DAD exit.)

PETER: Excuse me, Grandma, I think I'll go lie down. I didn't get a good night's sleep.

GRANDMA: Oh, don't go now, Peter. I'm just about to introduce the Pirates.

PETER: Pirates?

CLARISSA: Oh, Grandma, were there really pirates? I love Pirates.

GRANDMA: Oh, so do I. And there they were - - looming on the horizon.

(PIRATES enter singing PIRATE SONG.)

CLARISSA: The meanest Pirates who ever lived.

GRANDMA: Very good, Clarissa.

PETER: Actually, I don't like Pirates and they don't like me.

GRANDMA: Don't worry, Peter. We can take them, can't we, Clarissa?

CLARISSA: Of course!

(PIRATES, PETER, GRANDMA and CLARISSA ALL fight.)

I bet you don't even read the newspaper, Grandma.

GRANDMA: I don't have the time. I'm too busy writing my memoirs.

CLARISSA: Oh, Grandma. I write, too!

GRANDMA: Good for you, Clarissa. You remind me of myself at your age.

PETER: *(HE has to hold off PIRATES as CLARISSA and GRANDMA talk.)* I don't mean to be rude to someone as elderly as yourself, Grandma, but could you tell us about some other adventure now.

GRANDMA: Why, of course, Peter. *(GRANDMA forces PIRATES off at sword point. PIRATES exit into closet.)* The truth is, I've had so many, I don't know if I'll have enough time to tell you all of them.

CLARISSA: You can stay in my room, Grandma, and we can tell stories all night long.

GRANDMA: Oh, good. We may have to stay up for days. Won't that be fun?

            (VAMP under PETER's lines.)

PETER: But, Grandma, you're old and everyone knows old people need lots of rest . . .

            (GRANDMA and CLARISSA get props from can.)

GRANDMA: Who would throw away this? It looks perfectly good to me.

CLARISSA: Do you think so, Grandma?

GRANDMA: Oh, yes. We can make good use of this. And this, too.

PETER: And this room - - look at it, Grandma, and right now it looks good . . . you should have seen it this morning . . .

(Room ends up a mess again.)

GRANDMA: The room can wait, Peter. We've got better things to do.

(MOM and DAD and CLOSET CHARACTERS enter.)

CLOSING SONG

MOM: *(With DAD)* CLARISSA WE'RE SO PROUD
THE SMELL HAS DISAPPEARED
AND ALL IS WELL
YOU'VE CLEARED AWAY THAT QUALM IN US
THAT GRANDMA'S FATE WAS OMINOUS
YOU'LL GET ALONG PHENOMEN'LY
YOU'VE GOT SO MUCH IN COMMON
SHE HAS LOTS OF ECCENTRICITY
AND NOT MUCH DOMESTICITY

DAD: *(With MOM)* CLARISSA, THANK YOU
I'M GLAD TO SAY
THE STUFF THAT STANK
YOU HAVE THROWN AWAY
AND WE'RE TOGETHER
LIKE ONE BIG FLOCK
BIRDS OF A FEATHER
CHIPS OFF THE BLOCK

PETER: *(With Mom and Dad.)* CLARISSA
AND GRANDMA
IT'S AWFUL, DISGUSTING
A NIGHTMARE
WE'RE RIGHT WHERE WE STARTED
IT'S HOPELESS

MOM and DAD: WE ALWAYS KNEW
YOU'D COME THROUGH

PETER: We did?

GRANDMA: THIS COULD BE A MAGIC LAMP
                OR ANCIENT CHINESE VASE

CLARISSA: AND THIS COULD BE AN ALIEN
                WHO LIVES IN OUTER SPACE

PETER: THERE MUST BE SOMEONE, SOMEWHERE
                WHO CAN HELP ME.
                I'M THE ONLY SANE ONE HERE
                AND I DON'T LIKE WHAT'S HAPPENING AT ALL

                (The following is all sung concurrently.)

GRANDMA and CLARISSA: A SHIP THAT'S FULL OF PIRATES
                OR A FAIR MEDIEVAL BAND
                IT DOESN'T MATTER WHAT
                IF WE'RE TOGETHER HAND IN HAND

MOM: CLARISSA DEAR YOU SEEM TO BE CONTENDED
                WITH THE TALES SHE INVENTS

MOM: BUT PLEASE REMEMBER
                THAT THEY DO NOT MAKE MUCH SENSE

DAD: THEY GO TOGETHER
                LIKE PEAS IN PODS
                I CAN'T TELL WHETHER
                I THINK IT'S ODD

MERRY MEN: FA-LA-LA-LA, TRA-LA-LA-LA
                FA-LA-LA-LA, TRA-LA-LA-LA

PIRATES: YO-HO, YO-HO-HO
                YO-HO, YO-HO-HO

ALL: SO WHAT

GRANDMA: IF THE ROOM SHOULD GET A LITTLE BIT MESSY

ALL: SO WHAT

GRANDMA: IT SHOULD MAKE FOR QUITE AN INTERESTING
                  STAY

MERRY MEN and PIRATES: THERE'S NO DOUBT ABOUT IT
                  WE CAN'T DO WITHOUT IT

CLARISSA and GRANDMA: We like it.

ALL: SO WE LIKE IT
                  WE LIKE IT THIS WAY

                        THE END